Participant's Notebook

High-
Performance
Mentoring

A Multimedia Program for Training Mentor Teachers

James B. Rowley, Ph.D.

For information:

Corwin Press, Inc.
A Sage Publications Company
2455 Teller Road
Thousand Oaks, California 91320
E-mail: order@corwinpress.com

SAGE Publications Ltd.
6 Bonhill Street
London EC2A 4PU
United Kingdom

SAGE Publications India Pvt. Ltd.
M-32 Market
Greater Kailash I
New Delhi 110 048 India

ISBN 0-7619-7525-X

This book is printed on acid-free paper.

03 04 05 06 10 9 8 7 6 5 4 3

Production Editor: S. Marlene Head
Editorial Assistant: Kristen L. Gibson

Contents

About the Developers

High-Performance Mentoring: A Multimedia Program for Training Mentor Teachers was created and coproduced by James Rowley and Patricia Hart of the University of Dayton. Jim and Tricia collaborated to produce the Corwin Press multimedia program, *Recruiting & Training Successful Substitute Teachers* (1998), and an audiotape series titled *Becoming a Star Teacher: Practical Strategies and Inspiration for Teachers* (1997). Other video-based teacher training programs produced by Jim and Tricia include *Mentoring the New Teacher* (1993) and *Becoming a Star Urban Teacher* (1995), both in national distribution through the Association of Supervision and Curriculum Development (ASCD). Jim and Tricia are dedicated to using audio and video technologies to capture and communicate the knowledge and wisdom of classroom teachers. In 1993, and again in 1995, they were corecipients of the Distinguished Research in Teacher Education award presented annually by the national Association of Teacher Educators (ATE).

CORWIN
PRESS

The Corwin Press logo — a raven striding across an open book — represents the happy union of courage and learning. We are a professional-level publisher of books and journals for K–12 educators, and we are committed to creating and providing resources that embody these qualities. Corwin's motto is "Success for All Learners."

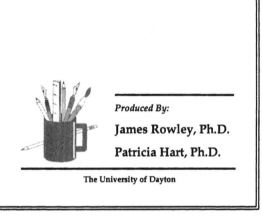

High-Performance Mentoring

A Multimedia
Program for Training
Mentor Teachers

Produced By:

James Rowley, Ph.D.

Patricia Hart, Ph.D.

The University of Dayton

Reflections

◆ *One thing I remember most about my first year of teaching is . . .*

◆ *One quality of a good mentor teacher is . . .*

◆ *One question I have about mentoring is . . .*

High-Performance Mentoring
Workshop Content

➡ Reflecting on Mentoring
➡ Knowing the Beginning Teacher
➡ Adapting Mentoring Practice
➡ Being the Professional Helper
➡ Coaching for Classroom Success

High-Performance Mentoring
Workshop Materials and Methods

Materials	Methods
✓ PowerPoint® Slides	✓ Personal Reflection
✓ Video Programs	✓ Group Problem Solving
✓ Reflection Guides	✓ Applying Theory to Practice
✓ Case Studies	✓ Role-Playing
✓ Inventories	✓ Clinical Analysis

Module 1

Mentoring:

Reasons and Rewards

Instructions

Reflect on your personal motivations for serving as a mentor teacher by completing the second section of the Mentoring Reflections Guide (page 5 in your notebook).

Time: 5 minutes

Video Program 1
Time: 9:00

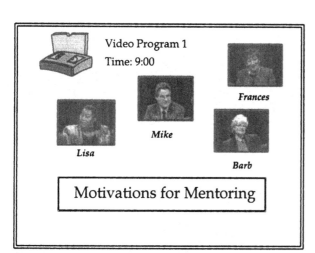

Lisa

Mike

Frances

Barb

Motivations for Mentoring

Working in your groups, take 5 minutes to discuss your reasons for becoming a mentor and how they are similar to or different from the mentors featured in the video.

Processing your . . .

Reflections on what motivates you to serve as a mentor teacher

The heart and soul of mentoring is an outgrowth of belief in the value and worth of people and an attitude toward education that focuses upon passing the torch to the next generation of teachers.

- Head, Reiman, & Thies-Sprinthall, 1992, p. 5

Mentoring Reflections Guide

Introductory Prompts

1. One thing I remember most about my first year of teaching is . . .

2. One quality of a good mentor teacher is . . .

3. One question I have about mentoring is . . .

My Motivations for Mentoring

1.	
2.	
3.	

Final Reflections

Module 2

Exploring the Principles of Mentoring

Background

In 1992, the Association of Teacher Educators' Commission on the Role and Preparation of Mentor Teachers published a report titled . . .

Mentoring: Contemporary Principles & Issues

- Bey & Holmes, 1992

The report identified ten *Principles of Mentoring* divided into the following three categories:

❂ The Mentoring *Process*

❂ Mentoring *Programs*

❂ *Selection and Preparation* of Mentors

The four principles of the *Mentoring Process* state that . . .

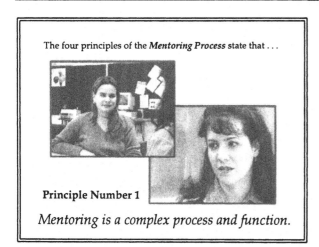

Principle Number 1

Mentoring is a complex process and function.

Principle Number 2

Mentoring involves support, assistance, and guidance, but not evaluation of the mentee.

Principle Number 3

Mentoring requires time and communication.

Principle Number 4

Mentoring should promote self-reliance in the mentee.

Instructions

Working in your groups, discuss the four *Principles of the Mentoring Process*. Record any questions, concerns, or insights you have in the right hand column of your Principles of Mentoring worksheet (see p. 11 in your notebook).

Time: 5 Minutes

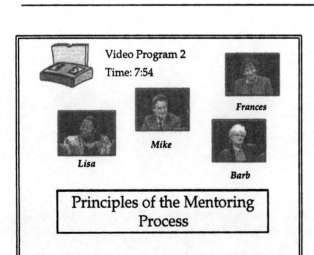

Video Program 2
Time: 7:54

Frances

Mike

Lisa

Barb

Principles of the Mentoring Process

Processing your . . .

Reflections on the veteran mentors' discussion of the principles of the mentoring process

---

The four Principles of *Mentoring Programs* are . . .

Principle 5: *Mentoring is bigger than induction.*

Principle 6: *Mentoring programs should involve collaboration with institutions of higher education, state departments of education, and teachers' bargaining groups.*

Principle 7: *The structure of mentoring programs should be consistent with school district goals.*

Principle 8: *Mentoring programs should be evaluated.*

The two Principles of the *Selection and Preparation of Mentors* are . . .

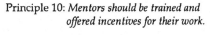

Principle 9: *Mentors should be selected based upon identified criteria.*

Principle 10: *Mentors should be trained and offered incentives for their work.*

Working in your groups, take 5 minutes to review the *Principles of Mentor Programs* and the *Principles of Mentor Selection and Preparation*. Use your Principles of Mentoring worksheet to record any questions you have about your mentoring program.

Processing your . . .

Questions, concerns, and insights on the *Principles of Mentor Programs* and the *Principles of Mentor Selection and Preparation* as they relate to your mentoring program

The Principles of Mentoring

- Adapted from: Bey & Holmes, 1992

The Mentoring Process	Implications for Practice
1. Mentoring is a complex process and function.	
2. Mentoring involves support, assistance, and guidance, but not evaluation of the mentee.	
3. Mentoring requires time and communication.	
4. Mentoring should facilitate self-reliance in the mentee.	

Mentoring Programs	Questions/Reflections
5. Mentoring is bigger than induction.	
6. Mentoring programs should collaborate with institutions of higher education, state departments of education, and teachers' bargaining groups.	
7. The structure of mentoring programs should be consistent with school district goals.	
8. Mentoring programs should be evaluated.	

Selection and Preparation of Mentors	
9. Mentors should be selected based on identified criteria.	
10. Mentors should be trained and offered incentives for their work.	

11

Module 3

Defining the High-Performance Mentor

Instructions

Reflect on your personal conceptions of the *high-performance mentor* by completing the Profiling the Good Mentor reflection guide on page 17 in your notebook.

Time: 5 minutes

Processing your . . .

Reflections on the qualities of the good mentor

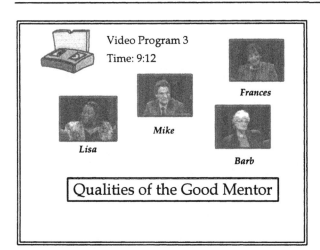

Video Program 3
Time: 9:12

Frances

Mike

Lisa

Barb

Qualities of the Good Mentor

Refer to page 135 in your notebook and find the High-Performance Mentoring Matrix. Take a few minutes to reflect on and discuss the performance standards identified under each of the six qualities.

As Clawson (1980) has pointed out, mentoring occurs in an interpersonal context that is based upon the degree of commitment and comprehensiveness of influence on the mentee.

13

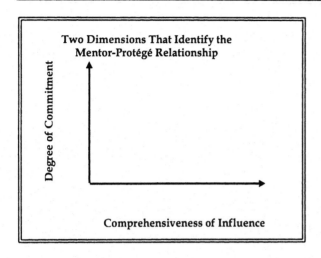

Two Dimensions That Identify the
Mentor-Protégé Relationship

Degree of Commitment

Comprehensiveness of Influence

Working in your groups, take 5
minutes to list at least five factors that
could cause a mentor teacher to exhibit
low commitment to a mentoring
relationship.

Processing your . . .

Thoughts on the various factors that
could contribute to a mentor
teacher's lack of commitment to a
mentoring relationship

Module 3: Defining the High-Performance Mentor

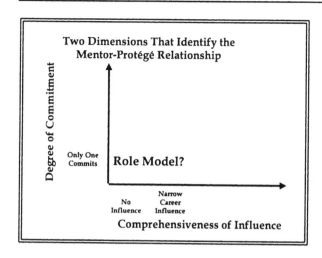

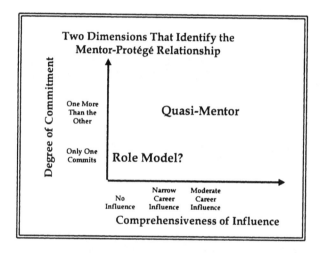

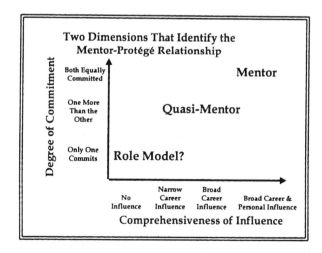

Working in your groups, take 5 minutes to list at least five factors that could cause a beginning teacher to exhibit low commitment to a mentoring relationship.

Processing your . . .

Thoughts on the various factors that could contribute to a beginning teacher's lack of commitment to a mentoring relationship

Profiling the Good Mentor

Instructions: Make at least two entries in each of the following boxes that reflect your thinking about the profile of the good mentor teacher.

Knowledge: What are the significant understandings?

Skills: What are the critical abilities?

Values: What fundamental beliefs are held and acted upon?

100 Things a Mentor Teacher Might Do in a Helping Relationship Model

1. Work with the mentee to analyze a lesson plan that did not work.
2. Remind the mentee of an important form that is due.
3. Introduce the mentee to other staff members.
4. Share an instructional resource with the mentee.
5. Go to lunch with the mentee to celebrate a teaching success.
6. Show the mentee how to access student records.
7. Help the mentee plan a strategy for solving a classroom management problem.
8. Avoid taking personal responsibility for the mentee's failures.
9. Observe the mentee's class to collect data on an instructional problem.
10. Listen to the mentee share a personal or professional frustration.
11. Demonstrate an instructional technique.
12. Collaborate with the mentee in planning/teaching a unit.
13. Make a video- or audiotape of the mentee for self-analysis.
14. Attend a workshop with the mentee.
15. Go to breakfast with the mentee once a week.
16. Encourage the mentee to reflect on a critical classroom event.
17. Advise the mentee on how to relate to another staff member.
18. Protect the mentee by maintaining confidentiality.
19. Alert the mentee to a behavior that you know may be self-defeating.
20. Confront and resolve an interpersonal conflict with the mentee.
21. Invite the mentee to a TGIF get-together.
22. Be self-disclosing with the mentee.
23. Assess the mentee's level of commitment and maturity.
24. Adapt supervisory practice to the mentee's developmental level.
25. Advise the mentee on the pitfalls of parent conferencing.
26. Take the mentee on a tour of the community or school district.
27. Counsel the mentee on a personal problem.
28. Refer the mentee to appropriate resource persons.
29. Encourage the mentee to participate in professional organizations.
30. Invite the mentee to systematically observe your teaching.
31. Hold and express high expectations for the mentee.
32. Be on the lookout for survival behaviors.
33. Give the mentee specific feedback.
34. Patiently answer the mentee's questions.
35. Laugh at oneself.
36. Model professionalism for the mentee.
37. Discuss a current educational issue with the mentee.
38. Help the mentee learn to write better test items.

39. Advise the mentee on how to better manage his or her time.
40. Share a personal success or failure.
41. Be congruent in mentoring beliefs and actions (walk the talk).
42. Remind the mentee of an important building or district policy.
43. Assist the mentee in keeping better student records.
44. Be positive.
45. Ask the mentee's opinion on a professional idea.
46. Brainstorm with the mentee a list of possible solutions to a problem.
47. Know the research on problems and concerns of mentees.
48. Share a professional article with the mentee.
49. Show the mentee how to fill out grade cards.
50. Model a disposition to inquiry.
51. Be open and honest with the mentee.
52. Encourage the mentee to try a new instructional strategy.
53. Hold a pre-observation conference with the mentee.
54. Help the mentee learn how to write better instructional objectives.
55. Advise the mentee of professional opportunities.
56. Display personal enthusiasm for teaching.
57. Positively reinforce a mentee's desirable behavior.
58. Check the mentee for understanding.
59. Use research findings as the focus of systematic observations.
60. Take a personal interest in the mentee's career development.
61. Don't take yourself too seriously.
62. Believe in the meaningfulness of your work.
63. Avoid sending mentees mixed messages.
64. Practice active listening.
65. Assist the mentee in reviewing instructional materials.
66. Provide the mentee with important information on a student.
67. Express the belief that all children can learn.
68. Know what it takes to build a trusting relationship.
69. Help the mentee understand issues on professional ethics.
70. Praise the mentee specifically.
71. Counsel another mentor on a mentoring issue or problem.
72. Encourage the mentee to attend a school athletic event or play.
73. Design and carry out an action research project with the mentee.
74. Help the mentee improve their classroom questioning technique.
75. Demonstrate for the mentee how to begin or close a lesson.

76. Appreciate the complexity of teaching.
77. Be sensitive to the mentee's nonverbal messages.
78. Share personal successes and failures.
79. Show the mentee how to more effectively use instructional technology.
80. Let the mentee know their problems and concerns are not unique.
81. Commend the mentee in front of a colleague.
82. Encourage the mentee to collect and analyze student feedback.
83. Model a positive disposition toward professional growth.
84. Express interest in the mentee's personal hobbies, travels, etc.
85. Advise the mentee on how to resolve an interpersonal conflict.
86. Arrange for the mentee to observe a colleague.
87. Protect the mentee from unjust criticism.
88. Practice patience.
89. Reflect on when it is time to speak and when it is time to listen.
90. Recognize that not all mentor-mentee relationships are made in heaven.
91. Help the mentee interpret the culture of the school.
92. Help the mentee understand the history of the district.
93. Script a lesson for the mentee.
94. Encourage the mentee to vary their instructional strategies.
95. Remind the mentee of the power of teacher expectations.
96. Value your own knowledge and experience.
97. Pursue excellence in your own classroom.
98. Accept change.
99. Accept the mentee.
100. BELIEVE THAT YOU CAN MAKE A DIFFERENCE!

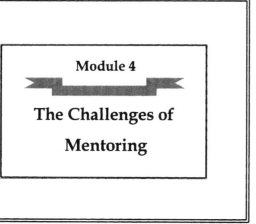

Module 4

The Challenges of Mentoring

Principle Number 1

Mentoring is a complex process and function.

Because of this complexity, mentor teachers frequently encounter a variety of problems and concerns.

Working in your groups, take 5 minutes to list your predictions of the most commonly reported problems of mentor teachers. List at least three.

Processing your . . .

Thoughts on the most commonly
reported problems of mentor teachers

Three Common Problems

Problem 1	Strategic Responses
I can't find the time to meet with my mentee. Our schedules are different, and we are both very busy. We just don't seem to be able to connect for any meaningful length of time.	

Three Common Problems

Problem 2	Strategic Responses
Some of my colleagues feel that my mentee is having some significant problems of one kind or another. They approach me as if they expect me to fix the problem.	

Three Common Problems

Problem 3	Strategic Responses

*I don't know what to think. My **mentee spends more time with another teacher**. They seem to be having meaningful conversations, and I guess I have some mixed feelings about that.*

Instructions

Reflect on possible strategic responses to the challenges of mentoring by completing the Three Common Mentor Problems worksheet on page 24 of your notebook.

Time: 8 minutes

Video Program 4
Time: 11:57

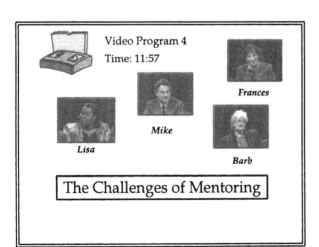

Frances

Mike

Lisa

Barb

The Challenges of Mentoring

Three Common Mentor Problems

Problem	Strategic Response(s)
I can't find the time to meet with my mentee. Our schedules are different, and we are both very busy. We just don't seem to be able to connect for any meaningful length of time.	
Some of my colleagues feel that my mentee is having some significant problems of one kind or another. They approach me as if they expect me to fix the problem.	
I don't know what to think. My mentee spends more time with another teacher. They seem to be having meaningful conversations, and I guess I have some mixed feelings about that.	

Questions From Practicing Mentors

The following questions were recorded on index cards and collected from mentor teachers at a mentor teacher support session.

How much do you push when you are faced with a reluctant mentee?

How much do you insist on working with your mentee when they feel totally confident in most areas and don't seem to need you?

My mentee wants background on an issue that has a direct impact on her responsibilities. The issue began before she was hired. Answering her would reflect negatively on a colleague, but failing to answer it may put her in a difficult situation with a parent and perhaps with that colleague. What to do?

When do you let go?

As a mentor, I sometimes feel guilty because my mentee is very competent and needs very little help. We have become good friends, and I am always there, but she doesn't need the help I expected.

Should I warn my mentee about a fellow teacher's attitude and predictably rude response before she approaches him with a student concern?

How do you handle an "I know it all" attitude?

My mentee's style of teaching is very "different" (uninteresting) from other teachers'. How do you suggest that he/she needs to change?

How impersonal can a mentor be and still be effective in the mentor/mentee relationship?

The teaching day can be so unpredictable, and there are times when I am struggling through "my own" day and then I am approached by the mentee for help. How does a mentor balance his/her own needs with the needs of the mentee?

I am very pleased with the whole experience. My question now is: What should my relationship with my mentee be when the year is over?

Module 5

Beginning Teachers:

Four Perspectives

Qualities of the
High-Performance Mentor Teacher

Commits to the Roles and Responsibilities of Mentoring	Serves as an Instructional Coach
Accepts the Beginning Teacher as a Developing Person and Professional	Models a Commitment to Personal and Professional Growth
Reflects on Interpersonal Communications and Decisions	Communicates Hope and Optimism for the Future

---

Four Perspectives

In the next three modules, we are going to explore the lives of beginning teachers from four diverse perspectives. We will seek to better understand entry-year teachers . . .

❑ As developing adults at different places in the life-cycle

❑ As adult learners

❑ As beginning professionals experiencing common problems

❑ As novice practitioners with developmental levels of concern

We will be applying these research-based theoretical perspectives to four first-year teachers . . .

Rachel

Richard

Maria

Mildred

Rachel

Personal/Professional
Profile

Age: 24

Assignment: 2nd Grade

Biographical Facts:

• Hired the day before
school started

• Married in August before
beginning her first year
of teaching

Richard

Personal/Professional
Profile

Age: 22

Assignment: High school
science including *Essentials
of Biology* for low-achieving
students

Biographical Facts:

• Highly recruited by the
school district

• Accepting his first job
required him to move to a
new community where he
had no friends or family.

Maria

Personal/Professional
Profile

Age: 23

Assignment: 3rd Grade

Biographical Facts:

- Maria was engaged
  during her first year of
  teaching and began
  planning her wedding
  for the coming summer.

- Moving to follow fiancé
  who got a new job

Mildred

Personal/Professional
Profile

Age: 42

Assignment: 2nd Grade

Biographical Facts:

- Employed as a social
  worker for 14 years
  prior to becoming a
  teacher

- Married to a teacher and
  the mother of 2 children

- Has lived in the
  community where she
  teaches for 13 years

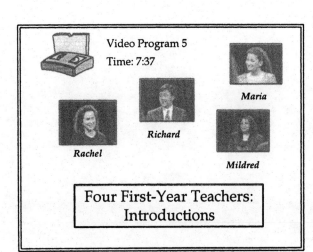

Video Program 5
Time: 7:37

Maria

Richard

Rachel

Mildred

Four First-Year Teachers:
Introductions

Module 5:   Beginning Teachers: Four Perspectives

Perspective Number 1:

Life-Cycle Theories of Adult Development

Many researchers have advanced theories that seek to better understand adult behavior in light of what is known about the types of needs people tend to have at various *age periods* in the human life cycle. The next slide by Gordon (1990) synthesizes the work of many life-cycle theorists.

- Gordon, 1990, p. 45

Age-Based Stages of Adult Development

Age	Stage
16-22	Leaving the Family
22-29	Getting Into the World
29-32	Age 30 Transition
32-35	Rooting
35-40	Becoming One's Own Person
40-43	Midlife Transition
43-50	Restabilization
50-65	Preretirement

Leaving the Family Stage

Persons in this age category often struggle with the tension between dependence on family and the strong need to think and act independently. They are asking questions such as *Who am I?* and *How do I fit into the adult world?*

- Krupp, 1981, p. 16

Getting Into the World **stage**

Persons in this period want to demonstrate their competence and independence as quickly as possible. Teaching is perceived as a career to *help the kids* and *transmit information,* and thus the teacher's competence is directly related to the children learning accurately and quickly. If this does not come about, the *twenties* teacher may well perceive himself or herself to have failed.

- Krupp, 1981, p. 30

Leaving the Family & Getting Into the World

Rachel, 24, experienced her first year of marriage along with her first year of teaching.

Maria, 23, left her first teaching job at the end of the year to follow her fiancé who began medical school in another part of the state.

Richard, 22, accepted a position that took him away from family and friends. He left the school district at the end of the year to move closer to his parents.

Midlife Transition

Mildred, 41, transitioned to teaching after working for 13 years as a social worker. She has lived in the community for 13 years and is married to a teacher and has 2 adult children.

Perspective Number 2:

Adult Learning Theory

A second perspective mentors can take on beginning teachers is to view them as *adult learners*. One of the leading researchers and writers in the field of adult learning is Malcolm Knowles. Knowles (1978) identified five basic principles of adult learning. Each principle has important implications for mentoring the beginning teacher.

Five Principles of Adult Learning

1. Adults are motivated to learn as they experience needs and interests.
2. Adults' orientation to learning is life-centered.
3. Experience is the richest resource for adult learning.
4. Adults have a deep need to be self-directing.
5. Individual differences between people increase with age.

- Knowles, 1978

Instructions

Reflect on the principles of adult learning and their implications for high-performance mentoring by working in your groups to complete the Beginning Teachers as Adult Learners reflection guide on page 33 in your notebook.

Time: 8 minutes

Processing your . . .

Reflections on the principles
of adult learning and their
implications for mentoring

Beginning Teachers
as Adult Learners

Principles of Adult Learning	Implications for Mentoring
1. *Adults are motivated to learn as they experience needs and interests.*	
2. *Adults' orientation to learning is life-centered.*	
3. *Experience is the richest resource for adult learning.*	
4. *Adults have a deep need to be self-directing.*	
5. *Individual differences between people increase with age.*	

Module 6

Common Problems of
Beginning Teachers

Beginning Teachers:
Four Perspectives

- ❑ As developing adults at different places in the life cycle
- ❑ As adult learners
- ❑ As beginning professionals experiencing common problems
- ❑ As novice practitioners with developmental levels of concern

---

Perceived Problems of
Beginning Teachers

A study by Veenman (1986) synthesized the research on beginning teachers and identified the problems they most commonly report during their first year of teaching.

Let's Play

The Family Feud

SURVEY QUESTION:

What are the most commonly reported problems of beginning teachers *as reported by beginning teachers?*

Working in your groups, take 10 minutes to list the eight most commonly reported problems of beginning teachers in the left-hand column of the worksheet on page 38 of your notebook. After you have your list of eight, prioritize the top three problems.

Module 6: Common Problems of Beginning Teachers

Important Reminder:

You are being asked to predict what beginning teachers report when asked to describe the problems they are having. Such answers may be different than those one might get if you asked veteran teachers to describe the problems of first-year teachers.

Number 1:

Number 2:

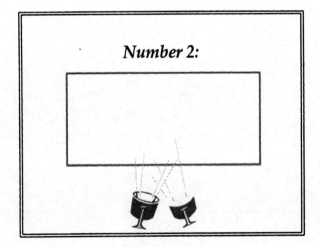

Number 3:

Instructions

Return to The Most Common Problems of Beginning Teachers worksheet. Record the results of Veenman's research in the right-hand column. Compare the answers in the left- and right-hand columns. Use the reflections box at the bottom of the page to enter any insights gained from this experience.

Time: 8 minutes

Processing your . . .

Reflections on the problems and concerns of beginning teachers

---

The Most Common Problems of Beginning Teachers

My/Our Predictions	Veenman's Research
1.	
2.	
3.	
4.	
5.	
6.	
7.	
8.	

Final Reflections

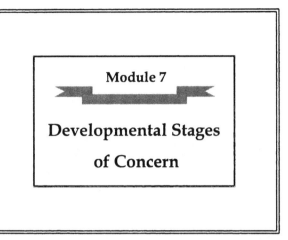

Module 7

Developmental Stages

of Concern

Beginning Teachers:
Four Perspectives

❑ As developing adults at different
places in the life cycle
❑ As adult learners
❑ As beginning professionals
experiencing common problems
❑ As novice practitioners with
developmental levels of concern

*Developmental Levels
of Teacher Concern*

A study by Fuller (1969) asked
teachers to describe their chief
concerns about teaching. The study
resulted in the identification of
three developmental levels of
teacher concern.

Take a minute now to quietly reflect on how you would answer the following question.

What is your chief concern as a classroom teacher?

Teachers' Developmental Levels of Concern Theory

- Fuller, 1969

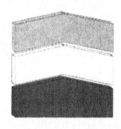

Stage 1

The Survival Stage

Stage One   Survival Stage

Teachers in this stage are primarily focused on . . .

<u>Self</u>

Some key *Survival Stage*
questions are . . .

- How am I doing?
- Will I make it?
- Do others approve of
  my performance?

People from whom many beginning
teachers seek approval . . .

✓ School Administrators
✓ Other Teachers
✓ Parents
✓ Students
✓ Mentors

Stage 2

The Task Stage

Stage Two	Task Stage
Stage One	Survival Stage

Teachers in this stage are primarily focused on . . .

Time

and

Task

Some key *Impact Stage* questions are . . .

- Is there a better way?
- How can I do all that is expected of me?
- How can I improve this?

Time Crunchers Frequently Reported
by Beginning Teachers

- After-School Activities
- Coaching
- Lesson Planning
- Extra-Duty Assignments
- Grading Papers
- Faculty and Other Meetings
- Graduate School
- Finding Instructional Resources
- Preparing for Parent Conferences
- Decorating the Classroom
- Tutoring
- Modifying Lessons
- Catching Up on Paperwork
- Classroom Cleanup

Stage 3
The Impact Stage

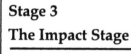 **Stage Three**   Impact Stage

 Stage Two   Task Stage

 Stage One   Survival Stage

**Teachers in this stage are primarily
focused on . . .**

Student Learning

Some key *Impact Stage*
questions are . . .

- Are students learning?
- How can I raise achievement
  levels?
- Is this meaningful to students?

Instructions

Working in your groups, brainstorm
specific things a mentor teacher
might say or do that would be
helpful to a beginning teacher in
each of the three stages of concern.
Enter your ideas on the Concerns-
Based Mentoring worksheet on page
45 in your notebook.

Time: 8 minutes

Processing your . . .

Ideas on what mentors can do to
support beginning teachers in
different *stages of concern*

Concerns-Based Mentoring	
Stage of Concern	**Mentoring Strategies**
Survival	
Task	
Impact	

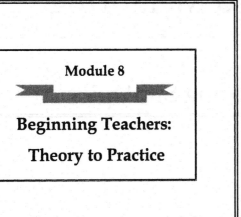

Module 8

Beginning Teachers:

Theory to Practice

Instructions

As you listen to the four beginning teachers discuss their first year in the classroom, make notes on their *reported problems* and try to identify the various *stages of concern* they experienced. Make your entries on the Beginning Teacher Observation Guide (page 48 in your notebook).

Video Program 6
Time: 22:32

Maria

Richard

Rachel

Mildred

Problems & Concerns of Beginning Teachers: Theory to Practice

Working in your groups, take 5 minutes to discuss your observations from the video. Prepare to share your insights with the whole group.

Processing your . . .

Insights on the *problems* and *concerns* of Rachel, Mildred, Richard, and Maria

Beginning Teacher Observation Guide

Rachel	
Richard	
Mildred	
Maria	

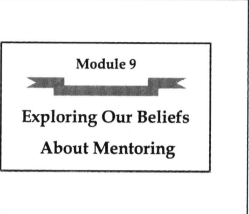

Module 9

Exploring Our Beliefs

About Mentoring

Qualities of the
High-Performance Mentor Teacher

Commits to the Roles and Responsibilities of Mentoring	Serves as an Instructional Coach
Accepts the Beginning Teacher as a Developing Person and Professional	Models a Commitment to Personal and Professional Growth
Reflects on Interpersonal Communications and Decisions	Communicates Hope and Optimism for the Future

---

Background

The inventory you are about to take has been designed to help you better understand the basic beliefs you hold about mentoring and how those beliefs might influence your mentoring behaviors.

Background (continued)

The inventory was adapted from the *Supervisor's Beliefs Inventory* developed by Carl Glickman (1985). It is a forced-choice instrument with no right or wrong answers.

Instructions

Take and self-score The Mentor Teacher Beliefs Inventory that begins on page 52 in your notebook.

Time: 15 minutes

When you finish scoring the inventory, feel free to compare scores within your group. Remember: There are no right or wrong answers or good or bad scores.

The Mentoring Beliefs Inventory

Nondirective	Collaborative	Directive
2.3	**2.2**	**2.1**

Source: *Developmental Supervision* by Carl Glickman, 1985.

The Mentor Teacher Beliefs Inventory

This inventory is designed for mentor teachers to assess their own beliefs about mentoring and professional development. The inventory assumes that mentor teachers believe and act according to three theoretical orientations to mentoring, but that one usually dominates. The inventory is designed to be self-administered and self-scored. Mentor teachers are asked to choose one of two options. A scoring key follows.

Instructions: Circle either A or B for each item. You may not completely agree with either choice, but choose the one that is closest to how you feel.

1. A. Mentor teachers should give beginning teachers a large degree of autonomy and initiative within broadly defined limits.
    B. Mentor teachers should give beginning teachers directions about methods that will help them improve their teaching.

2. A. It is important for beginning teachers to set their own goals and objectives for professional growth.
    B. It is important for mentor teachers to help beginning teachers reconcile their personalities and teaching styles with the philosophy and direction of the school.

3. A. Beginning teachers are likely to feel uncomfortable and anxious if their mentors do not tell them what they will be focusing on during classroom observations.
    B. Classroom observations of beginning teachers are meaningless if beginning teachers are not able to define with their mentor teachers the focus or foci of the observation.

4. A. An open, trusting, warm, and personal relationship with beginning teachers is the most important ingredient in mentoring beginning teachers.
    B. A mentor teacher who is too personal with beginning teachers risks being less effective and less respected than a mentor who keeps a certain degree of professional distance from beginning teachers.

5. A. My role during mentoring conferences is to make the interaction positive, to share realistic information, and to help beginning teachers plan their own solutions to problems.
    B. The methods and strategies I use with beginning teachers in a conference are aimed at our reaching agreement over the needs for future improvement.

6.   In the initial phase of working with a beginning teacher:
   A. I develop objectives with the teacher(s) that will help accomplish school goals.
   B. I try to identify the talents and goals of individual beginning teachers so they can work on their own improvement.

7.   When several beginning teachers have a similar classroom problem, I prefer to:
   A. Have the beginning teachers form an ad hoc group to help them work together to solve the problem.
   B. Help beginning teachers on an individual basis find their strengths, abilities, and resources so that each one finds his or her own solution to the problem.

8.   The most important clue that an entry-year workshop is needed occurs when:
   A. The mentor perceives that several beginning teachers lack knowledge or skill in a specific area, which is resulting in low morale, undue stress, and less effective teaching.
   B. Several beginning teachers perceive the need to strengthen their abilities in the same instructional area.

9. A. Practicing mentors should decide the objectives of any entry-year workshops since they have a broad perspective on beginning teachers' abilities and the school's needs.
   B. Mentor teachers and beginning teachers should reach consensus about the objectives of any entry-year workshop.

10. A. Beginning teachers who feel they are growing personally will be more effective than beginning teachers who are not experiencing personal growth.
   B. Beginning teachers should employ teaching methods that have proven successful over the years.

11.   When I observe a beginning teacher scolding a student unnecessarily:
   A. I explain, during a postobservation conference with the teacher, why the scolding was excessive.
   B. I ask the teacher about the incident, but do not interject my judgments.

12. A. One effective way to improve beginning teacher performance is for mentors to formulate clear professional improvement plans for beginning teachers.
   B. Professional improvement plans are helpful to some beginning teachers but stifling to others.

13. During a preobservation conference:
   A. I suggest to the teacher what I could observe, but I let the teacher make the final decision about the objectives and methods of observation.
   B. The teacher and I mutually decide the objectives and methods of observation.

14. A. Improvement occurs very slowly if beginning teachers are left on their own, but when a group of beginning teachers and their mentors work together on a specific problem, they learn rapidly and their morale remains high.
   B. Group activities may be enjoyable, but I find that providing individual guidance to a beginning teacher leads to more sustained results.

15. When an entry-year program meeting is scheduled:
   A. All mentor teachers who participated in the decision to hold the meeting should be expected to attend it.
   B. Mentor teachers, regardless of their role in calling for or planning the meeting, should be able to decide if the workshop is relevant to their personal or professional growth and, if not, should not be expected to attend.

Scoring Key

Step 1. Circle your answers to the inventory in the following columns:

Column I	Column II	Column III
1B	1A	
	2B	2A
3A	3B	
4B		4A
	5B	5A
6A		6B
	7A	7B
8A		8B
9A	9B	
10B		10A
11A		11B
12A	12B	
	13B	13A
14B	14A	
	15A	15B

Step 2. Tally the number of circled items in each column and multiply by 6.7.

2.1 Total response in column I   _____   x 6.7 = _____

2.2 Total response in column II   _____   x 6.7 = _____

2.3 Total response in column III   _____   x 6.7 = _____

Step 3. Interpretation: Refer to the Three Approaches to Mentoring worksheet on the following page to gain insight into your scores.

Source: Adapted from Glickman (1985), pp. 81-84.

Three Approaches to Mentoring

Interpretation

Instructions: The following brief descriptions of the three approaches to mentoring provide a general overview of each approach. After reading each description, reflect on your scores in terms of whether you believe they are personally valid.

2.1 Directive Approach. The product you obtained in Step 2.1 is an approximate percentage of how often you are likely to take a *directive approach* to mentoring rather than the other two approaches.

Mentor teachers with high directive scores may tend to believe that beginning teachers are best supported when their mentors provide professional direction that is grounded in their veteran knowledge and experience. Consequently, such mentors may feel most comfortable when providing strategic or technical advice.

2.2 Collaborative Approach. The product you obtained in Step 2.2 is an approximation of how likely you are to take a *collaborative approach* to mentoring rather than the other two approaches.

Mentor teachers who take a predominantly collaborative approach to the mentoring process may tend to believe that beginning teachers benefit most when their mentors relate to them as professional peers. Consequently, such mentors may feel most comfortable when engaged in collegial dialogue or collaborative problem solving.

2.3 Nondirective Approach. The product you obtained in Step 2.3 is an approximation of the degree to which you are likely to employ a nondirective approach to mentoring.

Mentor teachers who prefer a nondirective style of mentoring may tend to believe that beginning teachers profit most when their mentors provide them with the professional autonomy to find their own way and solve their own problems. Such mentors may feel most comfortable when listening to or encouraging beginning teachers as they seek their own solutions to professional dilemmas.

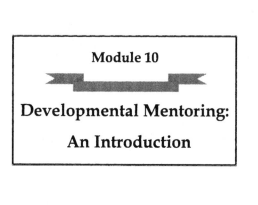

Module 10

Developmental Mentoring:

An Introduction

The Mentoring Beliefs Inventory

Nondirective	Collaborative	Directive
2.3	**2.2**	**2.1**

Source: *Developmental Supervision* by Carl Glickman, 1985.

The Mentoring Behavior Continuum

Nondirective	Collaborative	Directive
1. Listening	4. Reflecting	8. Directing
2. Clarifying	5. Presenting	9. Standardizing
3. Encouraging	6. Problem Solving	10. Reinforcing
	7. Negotiating	

Source: *Developmental Supervision* by Carl Glickman, 1985.

The Mentoring Behavior Continuum

Nondirective	Collaborative	Directive
1. Listening	4. Reflecting	8. Directing
2. Clarifying	5. Presenting	9. Standardizing
3. Encouraging	6. Problem Solving	10. Reinforcing
	7. Negotiating	

←————————————————————————→

HIGH   **Developmental Level**   LOW

Source: *Developmental Supervision* by Carl Glickman, 1985.

Developmental Level Defined

Developmental level, according to Glickman (1985), is determined by the teacher's motivation, experience, and competence.

In seeking to determine the developmental level of a beginning teacher, mentors might ask themselves . . .

1. **How motivated is he with regard to a particular task?**

2. **Is she *willing* and *able* to assume responsibility?**

3. **What skills does he have with regard to this particular task or problem?**

4. **What prior experience has she had in similar situations?**

Working in your groups, take 2 minutes to think of situations in which it would be appropriate for a mentor to employ a *directive* approach to mentoring.

When to Use Directive Behaviors

Directing   Standardizing   Reinforcing

Working in your groups, take 2 minutes to think of situations in which it would be appropriate for a mentor to employ a *nondirective* approach to mentoring.

When to Use Nondirective Behaviors

Listening   Clarifying   Encouraging

Working in your groups, take 2 minutes to think of situations in which it would be appropriate for a mentor to employ a *collaborative* approach to mentoring.

When to Use Collaborative Behaviors

Reflecting   Presenting   Problem Solving   Negotiating

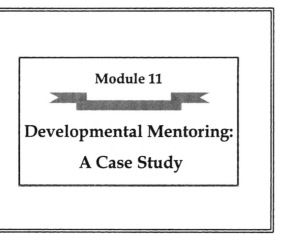

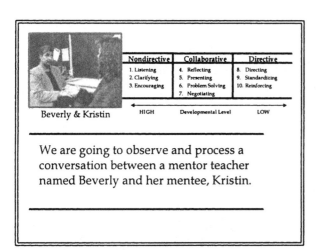

Nondirective	Collaborative	Directive
1. Listening	4. Reflecting	8. Directing
2. Clarifying	5. Presenting	9. Standardizing
3. Encouraging	6. Problem Solving	10. Reinforcing
	7. Negotiating	

Beverly & Kristin   HIGH   Developmental Level   LOW

We are going to observe and process a conversation between a mentor teacher named Beverly and her mentee, Kristin.

Processing your . . .

Thoughts on what type of an approach you hope to see the mentor employ based on what you know about Kristin

Instructions

As you process Beverly's interactions with Kristin, place tally marks (/ /) in the boxes next to each communication style you observe.

Video Program 7
Time: 10:11

Video Case Number 1:
Kristin and Beverly

Working in your groups, compare your observations of the conversation between Beverly and Kristin. Consider the following questions. Did you see the interactions in similar ways? Was the general tone of the conference nondirective, collaborative, or directive?

Time: 8 minutes

Processing your . . .

Reflections on the conference
between Beverly and Kristin

Video Case Number 1: Kristin and Beverly

Many mornings, driving to school in the predawn darkness, Kristin can hardly believe that her dream of becoming a teacher of children with special needs is now a reality. Yes, she is on the way to *her* school to be with *her* students. For a few fleeting moments she reflects on her college commencement ceremony and the unmistakable pride she saw that day in her parents' eyes. Her smile widens as she remembers her father's joyful reaction the day she received a phone call informing her that she had been selected for the Intervention Specialist position at Meadow Brook Elementary School, just six blocks from her parents' home.

Pulling into the school driveway, however, Kristin's thoughts take a sudden turn to less pleasant reflections. Seeing the lights on in several classrooms reminds her of the tension she is feeling with some of the teachers who occupy those very rooms. Being responsible for serving as the inclusion teacher for 14 students in six classrooms ranging from kindergarten to fifth grade is challenging enough without the increasing requests from several teachers for more of her time. Kristin has always prided herself on being an organized person capable of handling multiple tasks. This situation, however, feels very different and seems to be, as she recently described it to her fiancé, "on the border of being out of control."

Entering the faculty workroom, she is relieved to see that the room is empty and that the computer is available. Reviewing her new e-mail, she hesitates before opening messages from two teachers. Then, with two clicks of the mouse, each message confirms her fears. More requests for more of *her* time on *their* schedules. "There is only one of me and six of them," she quietly says to herself. "I can't be in six places at one time."

Frustrated, anxious, and a little angry, Kristin confronts the reality that she must finally address the problem. Her first thought is to walk down to the principal's office to share her frustration and seek some advice. Quickly, however, she feels uneasy about revealing the problem to her principal. Instead, she decides to send an e-mail to her mentor, Beverly, a veteran special educator who teaches at the intermediate school. "To: Bev. From: Kristin. Subject: S.O.S. Message: Hi Bev, If you can find the time today, I need some advice. Thanks, Kristin."

Developmental Mentoring Data Sheet		
N O N D I R E C T I V E	Listening	
	Clarifying	
	Encouraging	
C O L L A B O R A T I V E	Reflecting	
	Presenting	
	Problem Solving	
	Negotiating	
D I R E C T I V E	Directing	
	Standardizing	
	Reinforcing	

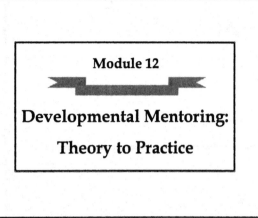

Module 12

Developmental Mentoring:

Theory to Practice

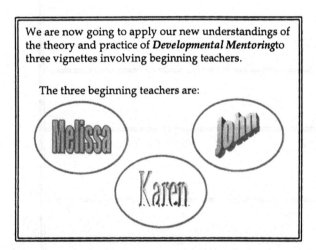

We are now going to apply our new understandings of the theory and practice of *Developmental Mentoring* to three vignettes involving beginning teachers.

The three beginning teachers are:

Melissa

John

Karen

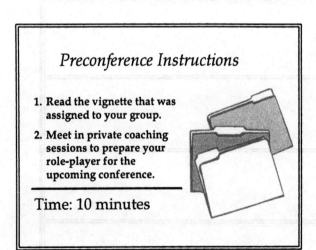

Preconference Instructions

1. Read the vignette that was assigned to your group.

2. Meet in private coaching sessions to prepare your role-player for the upcoming conference.

Time: 10 minutes

Conference Instructions

1. The mentor and beginning teacher role-players engage in a 5-minute mentoring conference in which the mentor endeavors to help the beginning teacher by employing the communication strategies discussed in the planning session.

2. The rest of the group processes the discussion by taking *descriptive* notes of critical or interesting aspects of the conference.

Time: 5 minutes

Working in your groups, take 5 minutes to process the conference. Process observers should begin the discussion by sharing their insights. Role players should then share their thoughts and feelings about the experience as well.

Processing your . . .

Reflections on participating in or observing the role-play conference

MELISSA

Melissa is a first-year teacher at George Washington High School, where she teaches general science to freshmen and biology to juniors. Washington High is an urban school located in a major Midwestern city. Melissa attended a prestigious university in the East, where she graduated with a major in biology and teaching certification. She is only 6 hours short of earning her B.S. in Secondary Education and is devoted to completing that second degree at a local college.

Julie, Melissa's mentor, is chair of the science department at Washington High and was part of the recruitment team that interviewed Melissa and recommended that she be hired. The team members, including the principal and the director of personnel, were all impressed with Melissa's excellent academic record in college as well as her leadership roles with two campus organizations. It is one week from Thanksgiving break, and Julie could not be more pleased with Melissa's professional efforts.

In fact, Julie almost feels guilty receiving the extra pay for her work as Melissa's mentor. Aside from keeping Melissa advised of certain "housekeeping" duties and introducing her to other staff members, she feels as if she has contributed very little to Melissa's professional development. "The kid," as she recently told her husband, "is something special." She is an extremely hard worker dedicated to planning, in Julie's words, the "most engaging" lessons she can. The word is out among George Washington students that Melissa is a good teacher who really cares. She recently volunteered to sponsor a new club dedicated to student service. Additionally, at the last department meeting, she presented a proposal for the creation of a new science elective course.

It has been almost a month since Julie and Melissa have had the chance to sit down and talk for any length of time. Julie feels the need to do that and is beginning to think about setting something up.

Notes:

KAREN

Karen is a first-year teacher at Laurel Oaks Middle School, where she teaches American history to seventh graders and civics to eighth graders. Karen is 39 years old and was a successful real estate broker prior to becoming a teacher. She attended night school twice a week for the last 2 years to earn her teaching credentials and began the school year with great excitement.

Unfortunately, Cassandra (Cass), Karen's mentor, has seen some of that enthusiasm fade over the first 12 weeks of the school year. One of the most difficult things for Karen has been managing student behavior. She readily admits that she just was not ready to handle the kinds of problems she has had to respond to. Cass and Karen have discussed this concern on three different occasions, with Cass responding to Karen's request for help by offering specific strategies she might want to try.

Today Karen asked Cass to come and observe her fifth-period class, the one that has been, in her words, her "nightmare." Cass was pleased with what she saw. Karen did an excellent job employing the strategies they had discussed in their prior meetings, and most of the students were on task and well behaved. There were still two students whose behavior was not quite where it should be, but Karen, in fact, had asked Cass to keep an eye on those students prior to the classroom visit.

The school day is over, and Cass is on her way to Karen's classroom where they have agreed to meet to discuss today's observation.

Notes:

JOHN

John is a first-year teacher at Sunnydale Elementary School, where he teaches fourth grade. John's mentor, Sharon, is an 8-year veteran teacher who also teaches fourth grade at Sunnydale. John graduated from a small Midwestern college located only 10 minutes from Sunnydale School. In fact, John lives in an off-campus house with three other young men who are in their final year of college. He readily admits that he loved college and campus life and enjoys being able to keep in touch with many of his college friends.

Sharon likes John's enthusiasm and creativity and is confident that he can become a successful classroom teacher. Nonetheless, she is concerned about a number of John's behaviors. For example, because their classrooms are adjacent to one another, Sharon is keenly aware that he has arrived late to school on at least six different occasions, and it is only mid-November. On four of the occasions, Sharon was able to cover for John and protect him from feeling the wrath of the school secretary. Another concern of Sharon's relates to John's less-than-consistent performance in the area of planning, especially for his science lessons. He has openly admitted that science is not his "strong suit." Finally, the ever-growing piles of ungraded student work piling up on a table in the corner of his room suggest to Sharon that he is not committed to providing students with timely feedback on their class work.

Sharon feels that, to this point in time, she has tried hard to encourage and support John by offering suggestions, sharing teaching resources and ideas, and making him feel part of the school family. Recently, she has heard other teachers at Sunnydale saying less-than-complimentary things about John. Sharon has decided to meet with John to discuss his progress.

Notes:

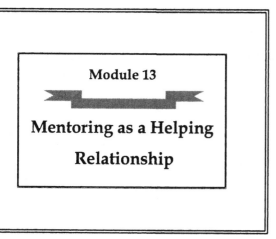

Module 13

Mentoring as a Helping
Relationship

Qualities of the
High-Performance Mentor Teacher

Commits to the Roles and Responsibilities of Mentoring	Serves as an Instructional Coach
Accepts the Beginning Teacher as a Developing Person and Professional	Models a Commitment to Personal and Professional Growth
Reflects on Interpersonal Communications and Decisions	Communicates Hope and Optimism for the Future

---

Mentor as Growth Facilitator

Lawrence Brammer (1993) has synthesized the research on *helper characteristics* that are known to facilitate growth in the helpee. Specifically, he has identified seven such characteristics.

- Brammer, 1993, pp. 38-44

Reflecting on . . .

Your prior knowledge and
experience in helping relationships

---

1. Mentor Empathy

"The way of being with another which is termed empathic . . . means temporarily living in their life without making judgments . . . to be with another in this way means that for the time being you lay aside the views and values you hold for yourself." - Rogers, 1958, p. 6	How can mentor teachers be empathic?

---

2. Mentor Warmth and Caring

"If helpers do not care, they run the grave risk of defeating themselves, or worse yet, of interfering with the growth of those they seek to help . . . People are much more likely to learn from people they like, respect, and feel one with." - Combs, Avila, & Purkey, 1971, pp. 235-236	How can mentor teachers communicate warmth and caring?

3. Mentor Openness

	How can mentor teachers communicate their openness?
"One learns to accept oneself from having been accepted by significant people. Openness to experience . . . and risk taking (result) from association with open, courageous persons." *- Combs, Blume, Newman, & Wass, 1974, p. 93*	

4. Mentor Positive Regard and Respect

	How can mentor teachers send messages of positive regard and respect?
"We cannot help people if we have no faith in their ability to solve their own problems. Respect develops as we learn about the uniqueness and capabilities of helpees." *- Gazda et al., 1991, p. 15*	

5. Mentor Concreteness and Specificity

	How can mentor teachers communicate in a concrete and specific manner?
"A key facilitating condition for . . . clear communication is the helper's attempt to be specific rather than general or vague. The effective helper models concreteness but also confronts the helpee about specificity and clarity." *- Brammer, 1993, p. 43*	

6. Mentor's Communication Competence

"Communication is a problem of interaction . . . It is necessary to be not only effective senders, but to also be attentive listeners. People must know how to listen." - Combs, Avila, & Purkey, 1971, p. 269	How can mentor teachers let their beginning teachers know that they are truly listening?

7. Mentor's Intentionality

"By a helping relationship, I mean a relationship in which at least one of the parties has the intent of promoting the growth, development, maturity, improved functioning, improved coping with life of the other." - Carl Rogers, 1958, p. 8	How can mentor teachers make clear their positive intentions?

Working as a group, take 10 minutes to develop a creative way to highlight a *specific mentoring behavior* that is representative of one of Brammer's characteristics. Refer to the Mentor as Growth Facilitator reflection guide on page 76 in your notebook to stimulate your thinking.

More specifically, prepare a 3- to 5-minute presentation involving some (or all) group members that makes a *serious* point in a *fun* way. To stimulate your creative juices, consider the following:

Skit	**Artwork**
Song	**Pantomime**
Poem	**Role-Play**
Puzzle	**Game**

Action!

Mentor as Growth Facilitator

1. Mentor Empathy

"The way of being with another which is termed empathic . . . means temporarily living in their life without making judgments . . . to be with another in this way means that for the time being you lay aside the views and values you hold for yourself."

- Rogers, 1958, p. 6

2. Mentor Warmth and Caring

"If helpers do not care, they run the grave risk of defeating themselves, or worse yet, of interfering with the growth of those they seek to help . . . People are much more likely to learn from people they like, respect, and feel one with."

- Combs, Avila, & Purkey, 1971, pp. 235-236

3. Mentor Openness

"One learns to accept oneself from having been accepted by significant people. Openness to experience . . . and risk taking (result) from association with open, courageous persons."

- Combs, Blume, Newman, & Wass, 1974, p. 93

4. Mentor Positive Regard and Respect

"We cannot help people if we have no faith in their ability to solve their own problems. Respect develops as we learn about the uniqueness and capabilities of helpees."

- Gazda et al., 1991, p. 15

5. *Mentor Concreteness and Specificity*

"A key facilitating condition for . . . clear communication is the helper's attempt to be specific rather than general or vague. The effective helper models concreteness but also confronts the helpee about specificity and clarity."

- Brammer, 1993, p. 43

6. *Mentor's Communication Competence*

"Communication is a problem of interaction . . . It is necessary to be not only effective senders, but to also be attentive listeners. People must know how to listen."

- Combs, Avila, & Purkey, 1971, p. 269

7. *Mentor's Intentionality*

"By a helping relationship, I mean a relationship in which at least one of the parties has the intent of promoting the growth, development, maturity, improved functioning, improved coping with life of the other."

- Carl Rogers, 1958, p. 8

Module 14

Types of Mentee Requests for Help

Four Types of Requests for Help

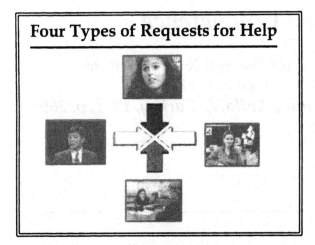

As soon as a helpee speaks to you, you begin to assess the situation. Even though you may not be aware of it, in your mind you seek answers to questions such as:

What does this person need?

What does this person want from me?

What can I do for this person?

- Gazda, et al., 1991

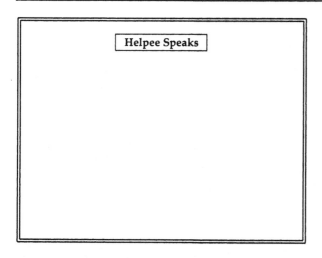

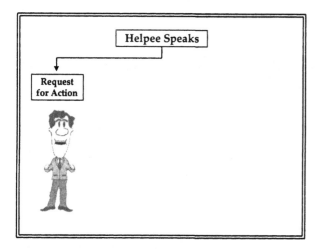

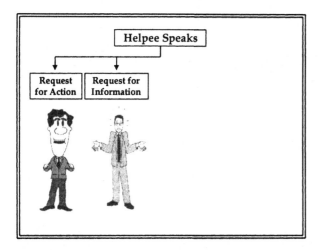

Module 14: Types of Mentee Requests for Help

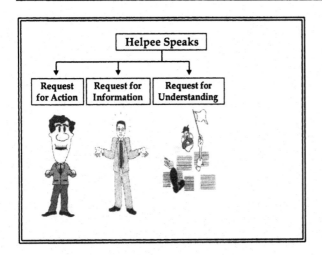

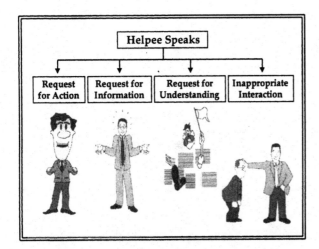

Types of Inappropriate Interactions

1. Gossip
2. Chronic Complaining
3. Inordinate Griping
4. Rumor
5. Solicitation of a Dependency Relationship
6. Encouragement of Negative Activity

- Gazda, et al., 1991

Module 14: Types of Mentee Requests for Help

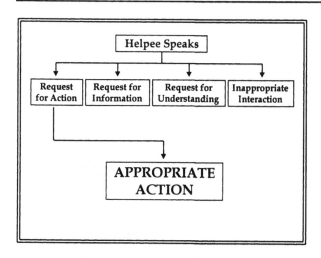

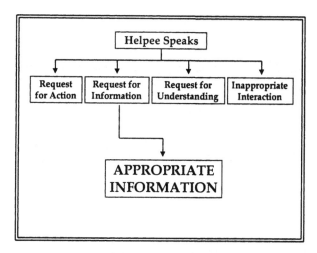

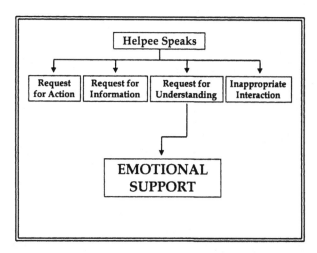

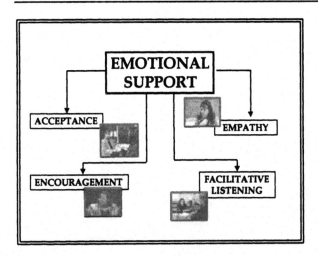

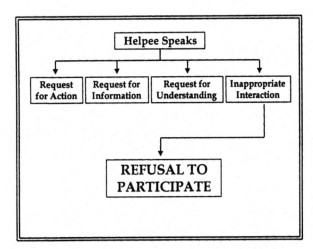

Instructions

Working in your groups, take the Request for Help Quiz on page 84 in your notebook. Try to reach group consensus on each item.

Time: 8 minutes

Processing your . . .

Answers to the *Request for Help Quiz*

1.
2.
3.
4.
5.
6.
7.
8.

Request for Help Quiz

INSTRUCTIONS: Identify each of the following items as a Request for Action (**RA**), a Request for Information (**RI**), a Request for Understanding (**RU**), or an Inappropriate Interaction (**II**). In some cases, you may feel that two answers are justified. This exercise is complicated because we are working only with the written word. In reality, there are many verbal and nonverbal clues that can help determine the true nature of the request.

_____1.　Mentee to Mentor: "What is up with Mr. Jones? Every time I pass his classroom, his students are out of control, and he is at his desk just ignoring their behavior. Is he burnt out or what?"

_____2.　Mentee to Mentor: "When a student asks me a question I don't know the answer to, I just panic inside. My professors told me not to worry and just say 'I don't know.' But I do worry because I feel I should know."

_____3.　Mentee to Mentor: "A representative from the teacher's organization met with me today during my plan period. I just don't know whether to join or not. I really don't believe in strikes."

_____4.　Mentee to Mentor: "Are we required to send home an interim report if a student is earning a D?"

_____5.　Mentee to Mentor: "Several of my students are really struggling with long division. They bombed my last quiz."

_____6.　Mentee to Mentor: "The copy machine was down this morning, and I have to copy my test for fifth-period. Can you sit in on my class until I get there?"

_____7.　Mentee to Mentor: "I was talking to Ellen yesterday, and she said that mentors are supposed to observe their mentee's teaching at least four times."

_____8.　Mentee to Mentor: "Did you see Mr. King's reaction yesterday when I offered my suggestion for parents' night?"

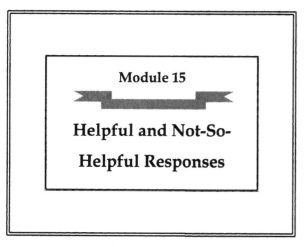

Module 15

Helpful and Not-So-Helpful Responses

Verbal Villains

Gazda and his associates (1991) have identified several *verbal villains* that represent ineffective communication styles.

- Gazda et al., 1991, pp. 50-55

Detective

Tracks down the facts of the case by questioning the helpee about the details of what happened

Magician

Tries to help by making the problem smaller or making it disappear

Drill Sergeant

Tells the helpee what to do

Gives orders based on what he or she believes is necessary to solve the problem

Hangman

Tries to help by pointing out how the helpee caused the problem by his or her own actions

Guru

Employs proverbs and clichés in an effort to share his/her wisdom

Historian

Prefers to use stories from his/her own past as a primary helping strategy

Sign Painter

Likes to help by assigning labels to people and problems

Florist

Is most comfortable providing emotional support and encouragement

Likes to maintain an optimistic point of view

Helper Responses

1. Detective
2. Magician
3. Drill Sergeant
4. Hangman
5. Guru
6. Historian
7. Sign Painter
8. Florist

Module 16

Helping Relationships:
Theory to Practice

Background

We are going to observe a
conference between a beginning
teacher named Monica and her
mentor, Soammy.

Based on the background reading:

**What type(s) of request for help do
you expect Monica to communicate?**

**What specific helping behaviors do
you hope to observe in Soammy's
mentoring responses?**

Time: 5 minutes

Processing your . . .

Reflections on the preobservation questions about Monica and Soammy

Instructions

As you observe the conversation between Monica and Soammy, record your observations on the Helping Relationship Observation Guide on page 93 of your notebook.

Video Program 8
Time: 10:37

Video Case Number 2:
Monica and Soammy

Working in your groups, take a few minutes to process your observations of the conference and prepare to share your reflections with the whole group.

Time: 8 minutes

Processing your . . .

Answers to the four questions from the Helping Relationship Observation Guide

---

Video Case Number 2: Monica and Soammy

Monica is a fourth-grade teacher who cannot believe her good fortune. Not only does she have her first *real* teaching job, but she also has a mentor teacher who, like herself, is a native Puerto Rican. Soammy has been teaching primary-age children at Edison Elementary School for 6 years. For the past 3 years, she has enjoyed mentoring beginning teachers like Monica as well as working with student teachers from a nearby university.

Mentoring Monica has triggered many memories—good and bad—of her own first year of teaching. In many ways, Soammy sees herself in Monica. Both attended private elementary and secondary schools in Puerto Rico before moving to the States to attend college, and both chose to remain in the States to begin their teaching careers at Edison. With so much in common, especially their Puerto Rican heritage, Monica and Soammy have developed a personal as well as a professional relationship.

Monica does not yet have a car, so Soammy drives her to and from school each day, a routine that has accelerated their friendship. Being able to observe Monica's before- and after-school moods has provided Soammy with valuable insight into the beginning teacher's daily experience. Over the last 3 days, Soammy has become increasingly concerned that Monica is struggling with a problem or issue that she is reluctant to share. So far, Soammy has chosen not to question her young friend about her sullen temperament.

Monica has recently been asked to be in a friend's wedding in Puerto Rico and is looking forward to the long weekend back home. Soammy feels that the opportunity for Monica to take a brief break from the first-year pressures could not have come at a better time. Her only regret is that she cannot accompany her young friend.

Today Soammy hopes to find an opportunity to uncover the cause of Monica's recent change in mood. She would like to provide any support that might allow Monica to travel home with a fresh perspective and renewed confidence.

Helping Relationship Observation Guide

INSTRUCTIONS: As you observe the conversation between Monica and Soammy, look for *specific evidence* you could use to defend your answers to the following questions.

1. What *request(s) for help (information, action, understanding, or inappropriate interaction)* did Monica bring to the conference? What evidence, verbal and/or nonverbal, supports your answer?

2. Were Soammy's mentoring responses appropriate to Monica's requests for help? Be prepared to defend your answer.

3. In what specific ways did Soammy model (or fail to model) Brammer's characteristics of *effective growth facilitators?* Refer to pages 76-77 in your notebook.

4. Was Soammy a *verbal villain,* or did she control the villains and use them in a helpful way? Again, be specific.

Module 17

Mentoring:

The Missing Analogue

In May, at an end-of-year support session, 25 beginning teachers were asked to describe what it was like to be supported by a mentor teacher.

Having a mentor teacher has been like . . .

Processing your . . .

Ideas on the ways in which the beginning teachers symbolized their experience

1. The beginning teachers' social-emotional needs were more important than their instructional needs.

2. The mentees were coached but placed greater value on other types of support.

3. Their mentors were not prepared or encouraged to serve in the role of instructional coach.

4. The mentoring program did not include classroom coaching in its expectations for mentors.

5. No time was made available to support the coaching process.

6. The local teachers' association prohibits mentors from observing their mentee's classroom performance.

7. The culture of the schools did not support having teachers observe each other's classroom practices.

Read The Law School reading on page 97 of your notebook. In your small groups, discuss the implications of the reading as an analogue for entry-year teacher support and development.

Time: 5 minutes

Processing your . . .

Reflections on The
Law School reading

The Law School

The Law School is very much a professional school. But it is distinctly not a vocational school. Students are not trained to perform many, or even most, of the tasks that its graduates may be called upon to perform as lawyers, and should not expect to be fully prepared to deliver a wide range of legal services on the day of graduation. Students may acquire or begin to develop some practical or technical skills and may gain confidence in their ability to perform as lawyers. Our practice-oriented courses and clinics provide, however, only an introduction to skills and a framework for practice which can only be defined through years of experience. The majority of our graduates join law firms where numerous opportunities exist for skill development under the supervision of experienced practitioners who share with the novitiate responsibility for the quality of service rendered. Michigan, more than many other law schools, seeks to provide students with the intellectual and theoretical background with which an attorney can undertake a more reflective and rewarding practice. It is felt that too much haste or emphasis on vocational skills, without a broader and more critical view of the framework in which lawyering occurs, runs the risks of training technicians instead of professionals.

Source: Pinar (1989), p. 12.

Module 18

Instructional Coaching:

An Introduction

Coaching Defined

Many dictionaries suggest that to coach is:

✔ *To Teach*

✔ *To Train*

✔ *To Tutor*

Coaching in the Performing Arts

Coaching in **Athletics**

Coaching in the **Professions**

Donald Schön (1985), who wrote extensively about coaching in the professions, argued that coaches are not just responsible for teaching technical skills.

> *They also must help their students learn how to make decisions in the indeterminate zones of practice.*

Instructions

Reflect on your personal conceptions of the "good coach" by responding to the questions on The Good Coach Reflection Guide on page 102 of your notebook.

Time: 5 minutes

Processing your . . .

Reflections on
The Good Coach
Reflection Guide

Stages of Skill Development

- Blanchard, 1993

Level 3	Level 2
Cautious Performer	**Disillusioned Learner**
Moderate Confidence/Adequate Competence	Low Confidence/Low Competence
Needs: Cheerleading and Encouragement	Needs: Emotional Support and Technical Assistance
Level 4	Level 1
Independent Achiever	**Enthusiastic Beginner**
High Confidence/High Competence	High Confidence/Low Competence
Needs: <u>Peer</u> Dialogue and Autonomy	Needs: Technical Direction

---

**Commonly Used
Coaching Strategies**

Focused Observation of Others
Demonstrations of Desirable Practices
Reflective Questioning
Reviewing Data About a Performance
Technical Advice/Suggestions
Emotional Support/Encouragement
Structured Self-Assessments
Referrals to Other Professionals
Recommended Practice Exercises
Personal Goal Setting

The Good Coach Reflection Guide

The purpose of this exercise is to help you reflect on your personal experiences with coaching.

1. *Identify someone you value as a personal coach.* To qualify, the person must have helped you improve your skill in some specific type of performance-based activity. Reach back to your childhood if you like or choose someone who is coaching you today.

   Coach's Name:

2. *Briefly describe one specific skill this coach helped you improve.* It could be your backhand in tennis, your ability to stop on roller blades, your acting performance in summer theatre, or your ability to make better omelets. **Be specific in a sentence or two.**

3. *List at least 3 personal qualities* of this coach that you believe contributed to his or her ability to help you develop competence and confidence in the skill area described above.

   My good coach was:

4. *Briefly describe at least two strategies* this coach used to help you improve your technical skills.

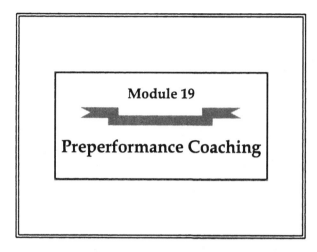

The coaching process, when done well, becomes an ongoing, cyclical process that can be expressed as a series of three phases.

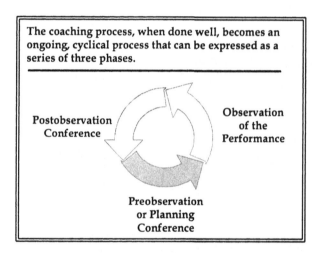

The coaching process begins with the *preperformance* or *preobservation conference*. There are two important sources of data that a mentor can focus on during this phase of the coaching cycle. They are:

1. The lesson plan

2. The feelings of the beginning teacher about the lesson

Module 19: Preperformance Coaching

In discussing the lesson plan, a mentor can seek answers to the following five *technical questions*:

Who are the learners?

What are the objectives of the lesson?

What methods and materials will be used?

Where does the lesson fit into the curriculum?

When and how will evaluation be done?

In seeking to understand the beginning teacher's feelings about the lesson, a mentor can focus on four *personal questions*:

How do you feel about this lesson?

Are there specific students you are concerned about?

Is there anything specific you would like me to observe?

Do you have any other questions or concerns about the lesson?

Melissa's Lesson Plan

Class: Biology
Grade: 7th
Period: 8
Topic: Plant Lab

Turn to page 106 of your notebook and find Melissa's complete lesson plan. Take 5 minutes to review the plan and discuss it with your group.

Instructions

In a few minutes we will observe a preobservation conference between Melissa, a first-year science teacher, and her mentor, Kevin. In preparation for that conference, turn to the Preperformance Coaching Reflection Guide on page 107 of your notebook.

Time: 5 minutes

Video Program 9
Time: 8:38

Preperformance Coaching

Processing your . . .

Reflections on the planning conference

Teacher's Name: Melissa Shearer   **Date:** 3/18/99

Subject: Biology   **Topic:** Plant Reproduction Lab

Grade: 7th   **Period:** 8th

Objectives:

1. Students will understand the parts of a flower and their reproductive functions.
2. Students will prepare a pollen slide.
3. Students will work cooperatively with a lab partner.

Learning Activities Plan/Sequence:

1. Brief review of material from yesterday
2. Introduction to plant reproduction lab
3. Pass out lab materials
4. Independent lab work with partners guided by written instructions and teacher monitoring of group work
5. Cleanup
6. Wrap-up and closure

Materials & Resources Needed: Plant Reproduction Lab worksheet, dissection kit, microscope, daffodils (1 per table)

Evaluation Plan: Answers to questions on the worksheet, observation of student performance during lab, multiple-choice items on upcoming unit test

Preperformance Coaching Reflection Guide

Technical Elements

Having analyzed Melissa's lesson plan, what additional information would you want to acquire in the planning conference? List your questions in the space below.

1.

2.

3.

4.

Personal Elements

As you watch the conference, observe Kevin to see if he attempts to gain insight into Melissa's personal needs and interests with regard to the lesson. Use the space below to note specific questions he uses to acquire these insights.

Module 20

Observation Methods:

An Introduction

Approaches to Making a Record of a Teaching Episode

There are many ways to collect data on classroom life. Literally hundreds of methods have been developed to systematically record different dimensions of teaching and learning in the classroom context. These different methods represent tools available to any mentor wishing to improve their work as an *instructional coach*.

Types of Observation Tools

1. Video- and Audiotaping
2. Visual Diagramming
3. Coding
4. Frequency Counting
5. Scripting

Video- and Audiotaping

Excellent tool for recording:
- verbal and nonverbal behaviors
- teacher and student interactions, and many other important factors

Tips:

Don't overlook the power of audio-taping!

Reminder: People vary widely in comfort level of being videotaped.

Reminder: You don't have to do the taping or even watch the tape to have it be an effective tool.

Visual Diagramming

Excellent tool for recording:
- teacher movement
- verbal interactions
- physical environment
- disciplinary behaviors

Tip:

It is easy to create your own system tailored to focus on the needs and interests of the beginning teacher.

Coding

Excellent tool for recording:
- specific behaviors of interest such as teacher praise
- questioning techniques, teacher clarity, and teacher responses to misbehavior

Tip:

An excellent source of coding instruments can be found in *Looking in Classrooms* by Brophy and Good (1991).

Teacher Responses to Student Answers

Codes

A = Praise
B = Neutral response
C = Moves to next?
D = Asks follow-up?

1. A
2. A
3. B
4. D
5. A
6. B

Frequencies Counting

Excellent tool for recording:

- equity issues
- verbal interaction patterns
- teacher questions
- anything else that happens in a classroom that is worth counting

Tip:

This approach offers a non-threatening way for mentors to bring attention to nervous habits or repetitive behaviors that may be distracting to students.

Boys //// ///
Girls ///

Interruptions ///

Divergent ////
Convergent //// //

Scripting

Excellent tool for recording:

- classroom events from a more holistic perspective
- for focusing on identified elements of good teaching

Tip:

Like the development of any skill, scripting takes practice. Many teachers who initially find it difficult will eventually become comfortable and proficient with practice.

9:20   T called the class to order and asked students to form their cooperative learning teams. Without further instruction, students reorganized their desks into small circles of four desks each.

9:23   T asked the materials person from each group to pick up a stack of papers from her desk.

Although the preceding types of classroom observation tools use different data collection techniques, they all have a common purpose:

To create a *nonjudgmental record* of the teacher's performance that can act as a *mirror* that as accurately as possible reflects the teacher's experience

Module 20: Observation Methods: An Introduction

> ## Reasons for Beginning With Objective Observations
>
> ---
>
> - Avoid the interpretation trap
> - Avoid beginning with unsolicited advice
> - Avoid rushing to judgment
> - Avoid making the mentee defensive
>
> ---

> ## Some Positive Reasons
>
> ---
>
> - Focus on the data, not the person
> - Promote beginning teacher's reflection
> - Stimulate meaningful conversation
> - Set a professional atmosphere
>
> ---

Module 21

Classroom Teaching

Episode: Clinical Practice

For the lesson we are about to observe, we are going to employ *scripting* for the following reasons:

1. It is an excellent tool to use for a first-time observation of a beginning teacher.

2. It requires no special forms, charts, or techniques.

3. It permits the coach to take a broad view of the teaching episode.

There are two basic scripting methods.

The Open-Ended Narrative

The Focused Narrative

The Open-Ended Narrative

The observer records the events of the lesson as they occur. The result is a chronological story of the teaching episode as it unfolded. One advantage of this approach is that the teacher reflects on the lesson in a linear time-driven fashion.

The Focused Narrative

The observer records classroom events because they fall into specific categories of interest. The categories can be defined by a framework for effective practice or can be negotiated by the mentor and the beginning teacher.

Tips for Creating a Quality Script

Regardless of the technology you use

Make sure your comments are DESCRIPTIVE rather than JUDGMENTAL.

That means avoiding praise as well as criticism!!!

If you use abbreviations or symbols, provide a legend.

T introduced the lesson at 10:05. MS asked T for clarification on HW. T ignored MS and proceeded to hand out the pretest.

T = teacher
MS = male student
HW = homework

Refrain from making suggestions.

Suggestions imply judgment. You will have the opportunity to offer suggestions later.

Instructions

Turn to page 118 in your notebook. Read the Sample Open-Ended Narrative, and underline or highlight any portions of the script that you feel are judgmental.

Time: 8 minutes

Processing your . . .

Reflections on the sample open-ended narrative script

Instructions

1. Divide each group into two subgroups, one of which will write an open-ended script and the other of which will write a focused script.

2. Prepare a piece of blank paper for your form of scripting.

Time: 5 minutes

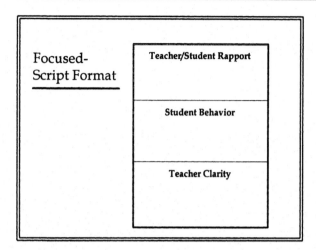

Focused-
Script Format

Teacher/Student Rapport

Student Behavior

Teacher Clarity

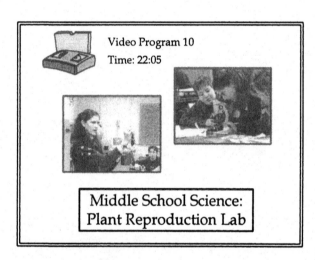

Video Program 10
Time: 22:05

Middle School Science:
Plant Reproduction Lab

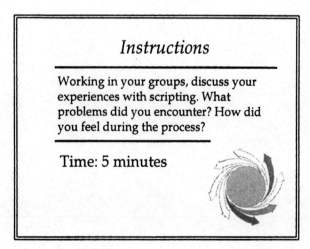

Instructions

Working in your groups, discuss your
experiences with scripting. What
problems did you encounter? How did
you feel during the process?

Time: 5 minutes

Processing your . . .

Reflections on the scripting
experience

Sample Open-Ended Narrative

The teacher is a traveling teacher. She arrived at the room at 9:01, put her book and pencils on the desk, and then went to the door. The students began arriving. They came in the room and sat at desks.

The bell rang. The teacher asked the first person in each row to get books. The first person in each row went to the bookshelf, got books, and passed them out. The teacher asked everyone to move up. Jeff (sitting in the last seat by the wall) said, "This is my assigned seat. I am going to stay." The teacher said, "OK." She told Tiffany (sitting in front of Jeff) to move up.

The teacher told the students to open their books to page 111. (This is a lesson in the different types of employment agencies, what they do, and the differences in them.) The teacher led a good discussion about the section. The teacher clearly wrote answers on the board as students gave them.

A girl came in late and gave the teacher a pass. The teacher did a nice job of continuing the discussion despite the interruption.

The teacher picked up her notes and asked students some excellent high-order questions as they looked at their books.

Jeff quietly made the noise, "Boom, boom, boom." The teacher ignored it.

There was a knock on the door. The teacher went to the door. She was given a note which she gave to Steve.

The teacher explained page 116 from the book and read some parts.

There was another knock on the door. The teacher went to the door and had a brief conversation with a male teacher.

The teacher gave worksheets to the first person in each row. The students passed them back. The teacher told the students these worksheets required the information they would need to fill out the resumes they will be doing later. Jeff walked to the teacher and said something to her. Then he put a paper on the desk. Steve put a paper on the desk.

The teacher read the directions for the worksheet and told the students the main information they would need.

The teacher asked Todd if he had a pencil. Todd felt his pockets and said, "No." The teacher gave him a pencil to use.

The teacher explained the worksheet and answered questions. The students worked on the worksheet.

The students talked among themselves (mainly pertaining to the worksheet).

The teacher explained something as some of the students kept talking.

Jeff walked to the pencil sharpener and sharpened his pencil. On the way back to his seat he talked with two students on the far side of the room. The teacher kept helping by giving ideas as the students filled out their worksheets.

The teacher gave instructions. Some girls were talking. The teacher said, "Shh, girls! Quiet please!"

The teacher stopped talking and put her book on the desk. Jeff put his book away. A girl put her book away.

Some of the students were talking or sitting instead of working. The teacher said, "We're not done for the day. Keep working." Todd got up and talked to students two rows over. The teacher said, "Todd, what are you doing? Get back to your place and to work." Todd went back to his desk to work. (The teacher was agitated.)

The teacher walked around the room and stapled each student's worksheets together. Three boys talked about cars. The teacher, losing her patience again, said, "Worry about this, not cars." Jeff and a girl in front of him talked about Jeff's girlfriend.

The teacher said, "We have four minutes left. Use your time wisely."

Heather took her book back. Jeff made noise with his pencil. The teacher said, "Quiet."

Jeff and others talked about the ninth-grade dance. The teacher said, "Be sure your books are on the window shelf." Some students put their books away.

Jeff got up to leave. The teacher said, "Wait." The bell rang.

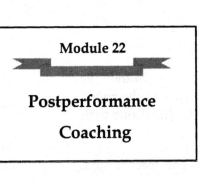

Module 22

Postperformance

Coaching

Qualities of the Effective
Postobservation Conference

Meaning is constructed by mentee and mentor.

The mentee is at the center of the process.

Dialogue is grounded in trust and rapport.

Conversation is planned but flexible.

Connections to past and future learning are made when appropriate.

Feedback is tailored to the needs of the individual mentee.

The next steps are negotiated between mentor and mentee.

Like a good learning activity, the typical post-observation conference has . . .

A Beginning	*How will I begin? How can I establish a positive tone? What questions will I ask? or What statements will I make?*
A Middle	*How will I use the descriptive data from the observation? How can I ensure that the mentee's concerns are addressed?*
An End	*How can I bring closure to the conference? Is there a meaningful follow-up planned? Is there mutual agreement as to the next step in the coaching process?*

Module 22:   Postperformance Coaching

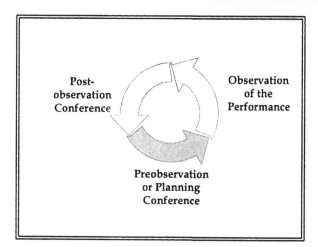

Post-
observation
Conference

Observation
of the
Performance

Preobservation
or Planning
Conference

Instructions

Working in your groups, prepare for the postobservation conference by completing the Postobservation Planning Guide on page 123 of your notebook.

Time: 8 minutes

Instructions

Prior to viewing the conference, turn to page 124 in your notebook and find the Postperformance Coaching Reflection Guide. Briefly review the instructions and items.

Time: 3 minutes

Module 22:   Postperformance Coaching

Video Program 11
Time: 12:06

Postperformance Conference

Work in your groups to discuss the post-observation conference. How did Kevin's approach differ from the one your group would have taken? How would you analyze the conference in terms of the seven items on the Postperformance Coaching Reflection Guide?

Time: 8 minutes

Processing your . . .

Reflections on the postobservation conference between Melissa and Kevin

Postobservation Planning Guide

In preparation for viewing the postperformance coaching session between Melissa and Kevin, answer the following four questions. *If you were in Kevin's shoes:*

1. What would your goals be for the conference?

2. What data from the script would you want to discuss?

3. Are there specific commendations you would want to give Melissa?

4. Are there specific recommendations you would want to make? If so, how will you communicate them? And what ongoing coaching support might you provide Melissa to help her find success?

Postperformance Coaching Reflection Guide

For each of the following items, place a check mark on the continuum above each set of paired opposites to indicate your interpretation of the postconference between Melissa and Kevin.

Meaning is constructed by the mentee and the mentor. Did Kevin allow Melissa to construct or coconstruct the meaning of the experience?

Mentor-constructed	Mentee-constructed

Mentee is at the center of the process. Did Kevin help Melissa feel that she and her concerns were the focus of the dialogue?

Mentor-focused	Mentee-focused

Dialogue is grounded in trust and rapport. Was there evidence that Melissa and Kevin are in an open trusting relationship?

Open dialogue	Closed/Constrained dialogue

Conversation is planned but flexible. Who drove the conversation? Was Kevin flexible in addressing Melissa's concerns and issues?

Structured/Mentor driven	Flexible/Mentee driven

Connections to past and future learning are made when appropriate.

Connections made	No connections

Feedback is tailored to the needs of the individual mentee. Did Kevin use communication strategies you felt were appropriate for Melissa?

Appropriate	Inappropriate

Next steps are negotiated between mentor and mentee.

No Next Steps identified	Next Steps negotiated

Questions to Promote Teacher Reflection

The following questions represent a menu of the kinds of communications a mentor teacher might employ in the postconference setting. Mentors may choose appropriate items from the following list or develop questions of their own. In preparing for postperformance coaching, remember to tailor communications in a manner that is appropriate to the developmental level of the mentee (see Module 10). The following questions are nondirective and collaborative in nature.

Regarding the mentee's reflections on the script or other observation record:

1. Have you had an opportunity to review the script of the lesson (or other observation record)?

2. Were there data from the observation record that you found of special interest? (of special importance? of special concern?)

3. Was there any data from the observation record that was not clear to you?

Regarding the mentee's general reflections about the lesson:

4. To what extent do you feel students were able to accomplish the stated objectives of the lesson?

5. How do you feel about the methods and materials you selected for the lesson? Would you change them in any way the next time you teach this lesson?

6. Were there any surprises? If so, tell me why you were surprised. How did you react to the surprise?

Regarding the continuation of the coaching cycle:

7. Is there an area of personal concern or interest that you would like to focus on between now and the next observation? Is there anything I can do in the interim to be of assistance?

8. Is there anything specific that you would like me to focus on during the next observation?

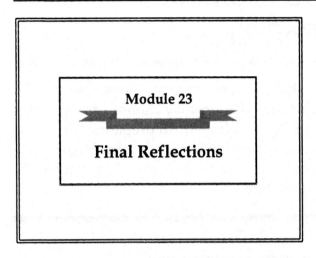

Instructions

As you listen to the final remarks
from the beginning teachers,
record any *final reflections* of your
own on page 128 in your
notebook.

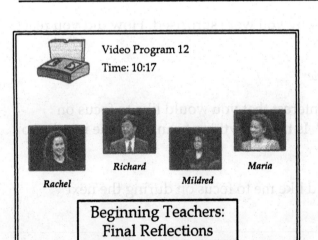

Video Program 12
Time: 10:17

Rachel   Richard   Mildred   Maria

Beginning Teachers:
Final Reflections

Processing your . . .

Final Reflections

My Final Reflections

Watching and listening to Rachel, Mildred, Richard, and Maria, I have the following thoughts about my future work as a mentor teacher . . .

As I reflect on my experiences in this workshop, I want to remember . . .

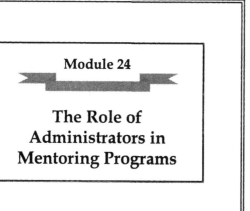

Module 24

The Role of
Administrators in
Mentoring Programs

Review the 10 questions on the reflection
guide and discuss them in your groups.
Be prepared to share any key issues or
insights with the whole group.

Time: 10 minutes

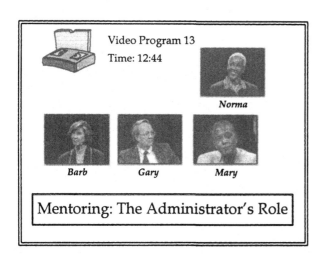

Video Program 13

Time: 12:44

Norma

Barb   Gary   Mary

Mentoring: The Administrator's Role

Processing your . . .

Reflections generated by the videotape

The Role of Administrators in Mentoring Programs

The following items represent 10 ways of thinking about the role of building-level or district-level administrators in a mentoring program. Use the questions as a vehicle for gauging your own level of support.

1. I am well informed about our mentoring program and its related policies and procedures.

2. I make positive public statements about the value of the mentoring program and its impact on the lives of new teachers.

3. I am enthusiastic when describing the mentoring program to new teachers in my building or district.

4. I participate on building-level or district-level committees that deal with the mentoring program.

5. I express my personal appreciation to the mentor teachers in my building or district in both private and public settings.

6. I endeavor to support the mentor teachers in my building or district by providing appropriate support (time, resources, etc.).

7. I respect the confidential relationship between mentors and mentees.

8. I do not use mentor teachers as a source of information about the performance of the beginning teachers in my building or district.

9. The mentoring of beginning teachers is one of the most important aspects of my work.

10. I believe mentoring programs for beginning teachers can be a source of professional development for mentor teachers as well.

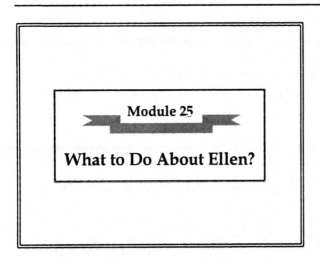

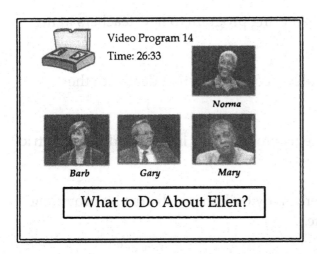

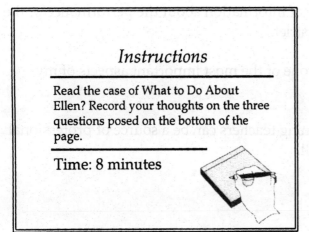

Processing your . . .

Initial responses to the case
of What to Do About Ellen?

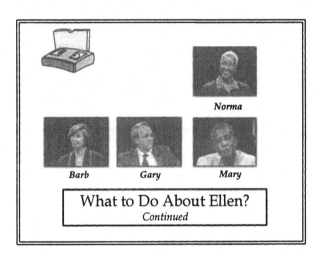

Norma

Barb   *Gary*   *Mary*

What to Do About Ellen?
Continued

Processing your . . .

Final reflections on the case
of What to Do About Ellen?

What to Do About Ellen?

Joan Carson is the principal of Apple Valley High School, where she has served as teacher and administrator for the last 12 years of her professional life. One thing Joan often says about her work in the field of education is that "there is never a dull moment. There is always some new problem or opportunity to keep life interesting." This year, Apple Valley High has a new Community Advisory Committee, a new computer lab, a new mentor teacher program, and seven new teachers.

In fact, Joan has recently been thinking a lot about one new teacher by the name of Ellen Jordon, who may be a potential problem. It is mid-October, and Joan has already had two veteran staff members approach her with complaints about Ellen and her apparent inability to control student behavior. She has just completed a hallway conversation with a veteran teacher who reported hearing a "lot of commotion and then seeing five boys run out of Ellen's classroom 5 minutes before the end-of-period bell." The teacher whose classroom is adjacent to Ellen's has complained frequently about the "distracting noise." To this point in time, Joan has taken no action.

Walking back to her office, Joan struggles with the question of "What to do about Ellen?"

Questions

1. What advice would you give Joan Carson if you were her colleague?

2. What would you do if you were in Joan's shoes?

3. What different courses of action are available to Joan? Try to identify at least three.

Qualities of the High-Performance Mentor Teacher: Knowledge, Skills, and Values

Commits to the Roles and Responsibilities of Mentoring	*Accepts the Beginning Teacher as a Developing Person and Professional*	*Reflects on Interpersonal Communications and Decisions*
☐ Dedicates time to meet with the mentee	☐ Endeavors to see the world from the mentee's point of view	☐ Reflects on what, where, when, and how to communicate with the mentee
☐ Persists in efforts to assist the mentee despite obstacles or setbacks	☐ Anticipates the needs of the mentee by thinking like a beginning teacher	☐ Adjusts communication style to the developmental needs of the mentee
☐ Maintains congruence between mentoring words and actions	☐ Understands the common problems and concerns of beginning teachers	☐ Respects the confidentiality of the mentor-mentee relationship
☐ Attends meetings and professional development programs related to mentoring	☐ Applies theories of adult learning and development	☐ Self-discloses regarding one's own professional challenges
☐ Models self-reflection and self-assessment as hallmarks of professionalism	☐ Models acceptance of diversity in others	☐ Models effective helping relationship skills
Serves as an Instructional Coach	*Models a Commitment to Personal and Professional Growth*	*Communicates Hope and Optimism for the Future*
☐ Employs the clinical cycle of instructional support	☐ Lives the life of learner as well as teacher	☐ Encourages and praises the mentee
☐ Values the role of shared experience in the coaching process	☐ Engages the mentee as fellow student of teaching and learning	☐ Holds and communicates high expectations for the mentee
☐ Engages the mentee in team planning and team teaching whenever possible	☐ Pursues professional growth related to teaching and mentoring	☐ Projects a positive disposition toward the teaching profession
☐ Possesses knowledge of effective teaching practices	☐ Advises the mentee on professional growth opportunities	☐ Avoids criticism of students, parents, and colleagues
☐ Models openness to new ideas and instructional practices	☐ Models fallibility as a quality fundamental to personal and professional growth	☐ Models personal and professional self-efficacy

Developed by James B. Rowley, The University of Dayton, Dayton, Ohio

Figure 1.1. High-Performance Mentoring Matrix

References

Bey, T. M., & Holmes, C. T. (Ed.). (1992). *Mentoring: Contemporary principles and issues*. Reston, VA: Association of Teacher Educators.

Blanchard, K. (1993). *Personal excellence: Where achievement and fulfillment meet* [audiocassettes]. Chicago: Nightingale-Conant. Side 7.

Brammer, L. M. (1993). *The helping relationship: Process and skills* (5th ed.). Boston: Allyn & Bacon.

Brophy, J., & Good, T. (1991). *Looking in classrooms* (5th ed.). New York: HarperCollins.

Clawson, J. (1980). Mentoring and managerial careers. In C. B. Derr (Ed.), *Work, family and the career* (pp. 144-165). New York: Praeger.

Combs, A. W., Avila, D., & Purkey, W. W. (1971). *Helping relationships: Basic concepts for the helping professions*. Boston: Allyn & Bacon.

Combs, A. W., Blume, R. A., Newman, A. J., & Wass, H. L. (1974). *The professional education of teachers: A humanistic approach to teacher preparation* (2nd ed.). Boston: Allyn & Bacon.

Danielson, C. (1996). *Enhancing professional practice: A framework for teaching*. Alexandria, VA: Association for Supervision and Curriculum Development.

Fuller, F. F. (1969). Concerns of teachers: A developmental conceptualization. *American Education Research Journal, 6*, 207-226.

Gazda, G. M., Asbury, F., Balzer, F. J., Childers, W. C., & Walters, R. P. (1991). *Human relations development: A manual for educators* (4th ed.). Boston: Allyn & Bacon.

Glickman, C. D. (1985). *Supervision of instruction: A developmental approach*. Boston: Allyn & Bacon.

Goldhammer, R. (1969). *Clinical supervision: Special methods for the supervision of teachers*. New York: Rinehart & Winston.

Gordon, S. P. (1990). *Assisting the entry-year teacher: A leadership resource*. Columbus: Ohio Department of Education.

Head, F. A., Reiman, A. J., & Thies-Sprinthall, L. (1992). The reality of mentoring: Complexity in its process and function. In T. M. Bey & C. T. Holmes (Eds.), *Mentoring: Contemporary principles and issues* (pp. 5-24). Reston, VA: Association of Teacher Educators.

Huling-Austin, L. (1992). Introduction. In T. M. Bey & C. T. Holmes (Eds.), *Mentoring: Contemporary principles and issues* (pp. 1-4). Reston, VA: Association of Teacher Educators.

Knowles, M. S. (1975). *Self-directed learning: A guide for learners and teachers*. Chicago: Association Press.

Knowles, M. S. (1978). *The adult learner: A neglected species*. Houston: Gulf.

Krupp, J. A. (1982). *The adult learner: A unique entity*. Manchester, CT: Adult Development and Learning.

Pinar, W. F. (1989). A reconceptualization of teacher education. *Journal of Teacher Education, 40*(1), 9-12.

Rogers, C. (1958). The characteristics of a helping profession. *Personnel and Guidance Journal, 37*, 6-16.

Rowley, J. (1999). The good mentor. *Educational Leadership, 56*(8), 20-22.

Schön, D. (1987). *Educating the reflective practitioner*. San Francisco: Jossey-Bass.

Veenman, S. (1984). Perceived problems of beginning teachers. *Review of Educational Research, 54*(2), 143-178.

Wolfe, D. M. (1992). Designing training and selecting incentives for mentor programs. In T. M. Bey & C. T. Holmes (Eds.), *Mentoring: Contemporary principles and issues* (pp. 103-110). Reston, VA: Association of Teacher Educators.

Suggested Readings

American Federation of Teachers. (1998). *Mentor teacher programs in the states* (Educational Issues Policy Brief #5). Washington, DC: Author.

Borich, G. D. (1994). *Observation skills for evaluative teaching* (2nd ed.). New York: Merril.

Costa, A., & Garmston, R. (1994). *Cognitive coaching: A foundation for renaissance schools*. Norwood, MA: Christopher-Gordon.

Darling, L. A. W. (1986). The mentoring mosaic: A new theory of mentoring. In W. A. Gary & M. M. Gary (Eds.), *Mentoring: Aid to excellence in career development, business and the professions*. Burnaby, B. C., Canada: International Association of Mentoring.

Huffman, G., & Leek, S. (1996). Beginning teachers' perceptions of mentors. *Journal of Teacher Education, 47*(1), 22-25.

Odell, S. (1989). Developing support programs for beginning teachers. In L. Huling-Austin, S. Odell, P. Ishler, R. Kay, & R. Edelfelt, *Assisting beginning teachers* (pp. 19-38). Reston, VA: Association of Teacher Educators.

Sweeny, B. (1998). *A survey of state-mandated new teacher mentoring and induction programs in the 50 United States* [Online]. Available: http://www.teachermentors.com

Zimpher, N. L., & Rieger, S. R. (1988). Mentoring teachers: What are the issues? *Theory Into Practice, 27*(3), 175-181.

Printed in the United States
By Bookmasters